Protecting the Pawn: Co-Parenting with a Narcissist

Chanel Jasmin Clark

Chanel J. Clark
PO Box 20486
New York, NY 10009

ISBN-9798572918106

Printed in the United States of America

Connect with the Spiritual Whistleblower

Life Coaching: ChanelJasmin@gmail.com

Youtube.com/SpiritualWhistleblower

Instagram.com/SpiritualWhistleblower

www.iloveSWB.com

Protecting the Pawn: Co-Parenting with a Narcissist

Chanel Jasmin Clark

I dedicate this book to all of the men and women who fight hard to protect their children from this silent covert abuse called Narcissistic Personality Disorder. The family court system is unfair, but God is watching over all of us and He won't let any of it go in vain. I send my love, strength and encouragement to you all. God bless.
~Love SWB

"Though my father and my mother forsake me, the LORD will receive me."

— Psalm 27:10

CHANEL JASMIN CLARK

CHANEL JASMIN CLARK

Protecting the Pawn: Co-Parenting with a Narcissist

Chanel Jasmin Clark

Table of Contents

PROTECTING THE PAWN

INTRODUCTION

Hello everyone. If you're here reading this, then I know you're probably fed up with the ongoing back and forth bullshit with your child's mother/father. You're sick of the unnecessary drama involving your children. There's a constant up and down pattern of passive aggressive communication when it comes to co-parenting with a toxic individual. Every time you try to make peace, the other parent finds a way to sabotage it. The gas-lighting and crazy-making are insane. All that you want is to make sure that your children have a healthy upbringing even though you are no longer with the other parent. When dealing with a narcissist, it's not that simple. It's complicated as hell; and unless you establish your boundaries early on in your child's life, you will spend the next 18+ years on an emotional rollercoaster. The worse part of it all, your children are now "inadvertently" involved in the all of this mess. Let me share my experience and hopefully it will give you the validation that you need to understand that you're not alone in all of this. There is an epidemic of dysfunctional households and broken homes created solely by narcissists.

Just to give you a little background on my experience with co-parenting with a psychopath; it was a hellish 15 years for me. My daughter's father impregnated me on my birthday, October 11, 1999. By the time I was three months pregnant; he abandoned me and went back to his other babymother. I figured that she was also a narcissist because he had abandoned her for several years and when she learned about me, she took him back and began smearing me. She believed all of his lies about me, disregarding the fact that he had already treated her and her kids like shit. When I had gone into labor, he videotaped me pushing my daughter out of my womb, then he took the video back to his babymother and they both watched it together. She was critiquing my birthing experience and made fun of the appearance of my vagina. What type of woman would shame another woman during her birthing process? A toxic female narcissist, that's who. Labor and delivery is a critical time where a woman could go into cardiac arrest giving birth to her baby. It really told me a lot about her nasty character and why her self-esteem was so low to attack another woman whom she knew nothing about other than the lies being told by a low life man who had previously abandoned her and her kids. Make it make sense!

Anyway, after he abandoned me and my daughter, he got a third woman pregnant right after. He disappeared and landed himself in prison after a few years. By the time he was released, a whole decade had gone by where he had missed out on my daughter's life. I attempted to give him another chance once he got out of prison to redeem himself as a father without either of us having to go through family court, but he fucked that all up. Of course I wasn't aware of what narcissistic abuse was at the time. My daughter's father also had a diagnosis of Bipolar Disorder and Schizophrenia that he hid from me. All of this information came out before the judge later on when I sued him for backed child support.

When my daughter was 14 years old, I allowed her to go visit with him because I felt she was of age to inform me of anything that went wrong while she visited with him. Bad idea. At that time, he had skipped out on most of her life and again, I tried to give him a chance to redeem himself with no established visitation schedule set in place. He lived in a small studio apartment and I was under the impression that it would be just he and my daughter spending time together alone. I later found out that his three other sons (2 which were adults) were also camping out with him. He had a 19 year old son who took my daughter to a wild party and got her drunk. Had it not been for me lurking on her Instagram page where she posted pics of her at the party, I would have never found out. I immediately contacted her father and he told me he had no idea and he kept apologizing for not keeping a close eye on her. The crazy part is, my daughter also suffers from Bipolar Disorder and her father treated her illness carelessly. I told him to bring her home or else I would come get her. The next day, he wouldn't answer his phone. He had taken my daughter out of the state all day and turned his phone off to avoid me. I went to family court and filed an emergency petition for supervised visitation and I also filed a police report for parental kidnapping. I took the papers to the police precinct near his apartment and the police called him and left him a voice message. They told him that if he did not surrender my child, he would be arrested. So he brought my daughter to the police station and they served him with the petition to appear in court to answer for my daughter being in a dangerous unsupervised situation involving drugs and alcohol. She is also mentally ill and a minor, so it really looked bad on him as a parent to have allowed this to happen on his watch. He never appeared in court. We haven't seen or heard from him in over seven years and it has been a very peaceful seven years. He completely discarded my daughter because he knew that supervised visitation meant that a third party would have to witness his manipulation tactics in front of my child. He rather treat her like trash and run a smear campaign about me to tell the world that I refuse to allow him to see his daughter (bullshit). He is allowed to see his daughter under court orders in the presence of her therapist or another professional. Game over. To this day, he still owes me over $150,000 in backed child support. I've already had him thrown in jail four times. He's the type of bum that rather serve prison time instead of doing right by his child. All of this to spite me because I will not allow him back into my life or inside of my home. I would rather allow a homeless man in my house, before my daughter's father.

I say all of this to say, that I sympathize with you. I have represented myself in the family court system, with the exception of two times. I was very fortunate to have judges who saw past his bullshit and threw him in jail. Every last judge we went before, hated his guts. I know that a lot of people have judges that are biased and favor the abuser. It's frustrating I know. So I wrote this book to help those of you that are battling these demons in family court because they want to continue to control our lives using our children. Narcissists are control freaks and they use their children as pawns to maintain leverage over their victims. Nobody wins, not even the children in these types of situations.

I hope this book gives you some peace as well as the much needed confirmation that you are not crazy. You have to be very diligent when protecting your child. You're not only fighting against your crazy narcissistic ex, you're also fighting against his family (your in-laws) and his new lover. His entire inner circle will keep tabs on you. He will do everything to provoke you into fighting with him just to frame you as the villain. You will be called a bad parent. The smear campaign will paint you as the bitter and lonely ex who also happens to be sad that the narcissist chose someone else over you. The mind games are relentless and it involves your child this time around. Whatever you do, please stand your ground and don't give up even if it feels like the narcissist is winning. The family court system doesn't play fair, but you must remember that we have an almighty God watching everything. The narcissist's days are numbered. May God continue to bless you and your family.

~Love SWB.

CHAPTER 1

WHAT IS A NARCISSIST AND HOW DO THEY ABUSE?

When it comes to co-parenting with a very toxic person, you're gonna do your best to keep the focus on the child. But what you're going to realize over time is the more that you try to make peaceful resolutions involving your child, the more difficult the narcissist will make it for you. Month after month, you see an ongoing pattern of push/pull, nice/mean, alert/distant dealing with a narcissistic parent. You begin to Google the behavioral patterns of dysfunctional co-parenting and the term "Narcissistic Personality Disorder" appears in the search engine. Then it happens, you begin reading numerous articles and you binge-watch YouTube videos; things begin to click inside of your head. All of the symptoms that you're reading about before your eyes, instantaneously fit the description of your child's toxic parent. Then it becomes clear as day: your baby father is a narcissist.

Before we can address the toxic co-parenting element, we must first address the root of the problem: NPD. What is a narcissist and what methods of abuse does one use to extract energy, time and finances from his/her victim?

A narcissist is an individual with an overinflated sense of self. A predator who has an insatiable need to feed off of other people's energy for the sake of filling up the bottomless hole in his/her heart. The narcissist lacks empathy, accountability, remorse and an identity. Manipulation and control are what drives a narcissist to jump from one victim to the next sucking each of them dry like a parasite. Everything and everyone who is willing to give the narcissist the much needed attention and adulation that he craves, will forever be great sources of energy fuel [Loosh].

Children, pets and anyone willing to be a slave, will make for excellent sources of narcissistic supply. The narcissist manipulates each victim by utilizing a toxic, repetitive cycle that he re-visits over and over again.

Love bombing. The first phase, is where the narcissist targets his victims with loads of romantic attention. If this is his child, he will spoil the child with money and gifts (*to compensate for the lack of emotional nurturing he cannot provide*). The narcissist swoops in on his prey and moves the relationship along really fast. Things become very hot and heavy because the narcissist does not allow his victim the opportunity to come up for air. It's a whirlwind romance that is set up to sweep you off your feet in order for the narcissist to land his hooks inside of you for the pre-destined kill. During this phase, he will bash his exes to make you feel adored. You suddenly are ordained the "new" soul mate in his life. You're having lots of sex around the clock. The narcissist is already planning your wedding and filling your head up with dreams of grandeur. What you're going to learn in the end is that all of it is a lie. Love bombing is a form of abuse that tricks the victim into believing that the narcissist is in love. The reality is, the narcissist doesn't know how to love, but he emulates the act of love in order to obtain narcissistic supply. Once the narcissist locks down his victim, he can proceed to move forward with the grooming process of breaking down his victim, slowly, sadistically and methodically.

Devaluation. The second phase, is where the narcissist completely stops showering you with love and affection. You will notice a shift in inconsistency with how things used to be. The compliments stop. The frequent sex stops. The flowers and cards stop. The attention stops. You blow it off and tell yourself that it's normal for relationships to slow down after things are hot and heavy for a while. You give the narcissist a pass and you find yourself working harder to keep the relationship together. Where the narcissist was once taking you out on nice dates and helping you pay bills, buying you nice gifts, you notice that you are now picking up the slack financially. Somehow, you are suddenly paying all of the bills, picking up the tabs on dates and buying the narcissist the things he needs. All of a sudden, the compliments stop and the complaints begin. Every time you share good news, the narcissist downplays it to make you feel insignificant. The gas-lighting begins and the arguments heighten. You feel like things are spiraling but as much as you love the narcissist, you are diligent to continue to fight to hold things together. You're isolated away from your family and friends, so nobody knows you're enduring this covert, emotional abuse behind closed doors. You were once so strong and you've allowed the narcissist to bring you down to his level. The narcissist begins to hint that there is a "third party" in your relationship, but he will introduce this person as a friend or co-worker. You have yet to learn down the line, that this is the very same person he has been cheating on you with the whole time. How did this all happen? How did the relationship go from pure bliss to constant arguing, belittling and drama?

Discard. The final phase is where it gets brutal. The narcissist is no longer hiding his true colors. He doesn't care if his actions are hurting you because he believes that you are too scared to break up or move on. He doesn't care that you find out about the cheating because he's going to project his guilt onto you and falsely accuse you of cheating. The name calling is savage. He is controlling your finances, your wardrobe, your social life and your self-esteem. You have completely lost sight of who you are and where you are going. The narcissist does not respect you nor does he care if you learn about his new lover (*the new supply*). He has been plotting to pull the rug from underneath your feet for some time now. The triangulation was meant to take you by surprise and make you believe that his new lover is much better than you are. Whether you dump the narcissist first or he dumps you, the break up is brutal and painful. If you are left pregnant, you now share that pain with an unborn fetus that is also being emotionally abused. To add insult to injury, you have no idea that the narcissist and his new lover are going to stalk you and torture you. You think the break up is permanent, but the narcissist is plotting to come back to continue abusing you when you least expect it. If you let him back in, he will start the abuse cycle all over again. Wash. Rinse. Repeat.

The goal of the narcissist is to seek out suitable victims who are empathetic, loving, giving and compassionate. Empaths with codependency issues from their childhood make excellent sources of supply because we are natural caretakers. You will stay stuck in a dead end relationship trying to fix a broken person who can't be fixed. That's why the narcissist deliberately trapped you in order to lock you down. The only way he could accomplish this was either through impregnating and/or marrying you (*his primary victim*) for the next eighteen years. He will continue to disrespect your boundaries by controlling you vicariously through your child.

CHAPTER 2

WHAT DOES PREGNANCY & MARRIAGE MEAN TO A NARCISSIST?

The narcissist has a warped sense of reality and doesn't view love the same way that an Empath does. In the narcissist's sick, twisted mind, he equates abuse as love and he must manipulate in order to control you in order for him to receive his kind of "love" from you.

If you happen to become pregnant and/or married to a narcissist, then you have no idea what type of mess you've gotten yourself entangled in. In your heart, you want to believe that despite the ups and downs of your relationship with the narcissist, that having a baby and/or getting married, will make everything better. Not so much. The narcissist has something up his sleeve: ***permanent entrapment.***

If you become pregnant by a narcissist, he will dump you during your pregnancy and pull away to tend to his other lovers. Why? Because you are now locked in. You are stuck for the next nine months and the narcissist will continue to torture you and abuse you, disregarding the emotional development of your unborn fetus. You have to remember that the narcissist is very sadistic, so the idea that you are carrying a child in your womb will bring on an onslaught of demonic, covert abuse like you have never experienced. The narcissist knows that your hormones are up and down; he knows that you have a severe case of morning sickness. Trust me, he doesn't care. He will continue to rub his new relationship in your face. He will continue to yell at you and call you a whore. He will continue to tell you to get an abortion (*reverse psychology to make you beg him to keep the baby*). He will continue to assault you and emotionally destroy you. Yes, all while you are pregnant. Going through a pregnancy with a narcissist running in and out of your life is disastrous. He is tormenting you with the full intent of not giving a shit whether the emotional pain is hurting your unborn baby.

When you give birth to your baby, the narcissist will reappear at some point in your life claiming to want his family back. This is false. What this means is that he either got kicked out of the new supply's (*the other woman*) house and he's trying to weasel his way back into your life and he's using the child to come see you, or he's either trying to see if you're seeing someone else. It is never about the child. The child is only a pawn piece to stay connected to you. The narcissist will use the child to keep tabs on your life, continue to have sex with you and monitor your love life. It's all about control and he will use your child every chance he gets to keep his foot in the door. He will also claim your finances and assets as his own, overlooking his financial responsibilities as a responsible parent.

The same thing applies with marriage. The narcissist is notorious for having "**Shot-Gun-Style**" weddings. He isn't into big weddings with large guest lists. He is on a fast-paced, whirlwind romance schedule, so he is going to want to get married at City Hall or either fly to Vegas and elope. The point is, he's focused on locking you down immediately instead of enjoying the whole experience of marrying you. He wants his **"Grade A Supply"** permanently on ice. The narcissist already has his side mistress/secret lover on standby, yes even on your wedding night. It's never about love. It's never about the vows you exchange before God. The narcissist is fully aware that once he marries you, should you want a divorce, it will cost you time, money and plenty of headaches to get one. You are now trapped in the venomous web of a narcissist. Pregnancy and marriage are his tools of preference to lock you down. The child is disposable.

CHAPTER 3

HOW DOES NARCISSISTIC ABUSE AFFECT AN UNBORN FETUS?

So listen, before I point out my observations about this, please note that this is based off of my collection of data and statistics. I'm basing this chapter from the numerous discussions I have had with many women who have a child with a disability and are co-parenting with a narcissist. It is my true belief that there is a significant connection between narcissistic abuse and developmental disabilities in a child. So this isn't speculation, but rather a plethora of undocumented experiences shared with me via my coaching sessions, including mine. I am a mother of child with a mental illness and developmental delays. I don't suffer from mental illness, however her father does. Once I started hearing multiple women come forward with their survival stories of domestic violence and the effects it had on their children, it all started to make sense. I saw a pattern between narcissistic abuse during the pregnancy months when the unborn fetus was in its developmental stages inside of his mother's womb.

When I spoke to each woman, I saw a pattern of disabilities in their children. Autism, Attention Deficit Hyperactive Disorder (ADHD), Cerebral Palsy, Oppositional Defiant Disorder (ODD), Bipolar Disorder, Schizophrenia and Cluster B personality disorders. When a woman is pregnant, should she interact with the father of her child and/or his toxic family, she will succumb to severe emotional abuse. During your pregnancy, the emotional stress that your body absorbs from being in the presence of a narcissist, will be transferred onto your unborn child. As your baby is growing inside of you, the baby is depending on you to stay healthy. If you are constantly being abused, then your baby is too.

Women have got to understand just how demonic and wicked this type of abuse is. Narcissists are sadistic and they don't care about children. They use pregnancy to trap their victims and once the child is here, the child will be used as a pawn piece to control the actual victim (you). In addition, your child will continue to be emotionally abused once he/she is born. The only difference is, the narcissist and his family will initiate the process to start grooming your unborn child to become disabled. They will attempt to program your baby at the onslaught of conception. I cannot stress to you enough to please stay away from the narcissist and his family during your pregnancy. Your unborn child will pay the price in the long term. I can also confirm numerous stories where the baby was still born (*dead at labor*) all due to narcissistic abuse.

I will never tell any woman what to do with her body. Abortion is a personal choice and it takes a lot of prayer and planning to move forward with having a baby. It's a hard decision to abort a pregnancy because the guilt will linger on your mind once you go through with the termination of the pregnancy. However, please consider the long term trauma and possibility of your child having a permanent disability and/or mental illness. There is a hefty price to pay when you co-parent with a narcissist and you're struggling on your own to take your child to therapy. I've been there and done that.

My daughter is now 20 years old, but she has had to go to therapy from the time she was 18 months old. She had inherited all of her father's mental illness. Eventually what started out as ADHD and ODD at an early age, later turned into Bipolar and Borderline Personality Disorder in her late teens.

The only thing I can remember is the abuse I endured when I was pregnant with her. The sleepless nights, constant fights, abandonment, other women and disrespect. He treated me like shit while I was pregnant. He poisoned my food while I was pregnant. He stole money from me when I was pregnant.

I feel so bad for putting my unborn baby through my trauma. If I had to do it all again, I would have completely moved far away from him and raised my daughter on my own, without the drama.

So the piece of advice I'm about to give you is priceless. This shit is not a game. If you become pregnant by an abusive man, please move far away from him. Cut him off until it's time to take a DNA test and then seek supervised visits. Do not text or take any of his calls. Until you have actually taken a DNA test, you are to remain in no contact with him. If he continues to harass you, please seek a restraining order until the child is born and paternity has been established.

Or you could actually cut him out of you and your child's life altogether. If your baby does develop a learning or mental disability, you can best believe that the narcissist and his family will try to stop you from getting the child therapy and treatment. They want to keep the child disabled and crippled.

A word of advice, you are better off cutting the narcissist off throughout your entire pregnancy to spare yourself the emotional torment and pain. You have to remember that your unborn child can feel your energy and is connected to you. Every time the narcissist abuses you, the risk of heart disease, learning and mental disabilities can develop within your child. You are under demonic attack and your baby will be exposed to it as long as you interact with the narcissist and his family. Any time someone can abuse a pregnant woman, trust me, that individual does not care about the unborn child.

My God, please protect your baby. The demonic energy that the narcissist gives off, will hurt your child permanently. Protect your child at all costs.

CHAPTER 4

YOUR NARCISSISTIC FAMILY & THEIR INFLUENCE OVER YOUR CHILDREN

If you're all caught up with having kids with a narcissistic abuser, then chances are that you have been groomed by a narcissistic parent. You have to understand that the "underlying" root of your childhood trauma is the main reason why you attracted a toxic, narcissistic predator into your life to begin with. It all starts and ends with your parents and how they program you as a child, to relate to others in the world. If your parents are narcissists, they will make you co-dependent and reliant on them for your emotional needs. They will not provide the emotional nurturing or support that you need to validate you as a human being. They will not teach you the basic survival skills to become independent in this world, because they want to keep you crippled and controllable. The person that you end of having kids with, is a reflection of your narcissistic mother or father. We repeat what we don't repair from our childhood traumas. How does this affect your children?

When you grow up around narcissists in your family, you have no idea how much of an influence they have over your children. Please realize that your narcissistic parent will also attempt to groom your children right underneath your nose. Your children will be spoiled with gifts used as tools to control them. The narcissistic grandparent will gossip about you to your kids behind your back. Your parenting style will be ignored and downplayed. Everything to drive a wedge between you and your child will come into play. If I can offer a piece of advice, when you have kids, you have to move far away from your narcissistic parent, or else they will attempt to rule over you by stealing your children away. Don't put your kids through that again or you can risk having you child turn against you due to the narcissistic parents grooming. If you are successful in keeping your children away from your toxic parents, then you and your children will be discarded. Remember, if narcissists can't control you, they will invalidate you by pretending you don't exist. Allow yourself the freedom to keep your kids away from that toxic environment. Your parents do not love your kids, nor should you force your kids to love them. And if you live with your parents, get the fuck out and get your own apartment or you will eventually pay the price down the line. Keep your kids away from your narcissistic parents or suffer the consequences later!

CHAPTER 5

THE NARCISSIST TRIANGULATES HIS CHILD AGAINST OTHERS

This may be a hard pill to swallow, but I'm here to give it to you raw. When I'm coaching my clients, I don't sugar coat because the narcissist has been lying to you enough. You deserve the truth. The narcissist does not love the child you share in common. The child means nothing to him He will use the child as a trophy piece to bring further attention to himself and/or to make others jealous of him. This is called *"Triangulation."* Let me explain.

Narcissists lack empathy so it is not possible for them to love anyone, not even their children. There is no emotional connection to anyone. The child is merely a pawn to be used as a binder/buffer to stay connected to you (*the primary victim*); to constantly intrude on your personal space. If you demand the narcissist respect your boundaries, he will accuse you of alienating him from his child and he will even threaten to sue you for parental alienation in family court. The child is his meal ticket and he will exploit the child every chance he can get.

Yes it may seem like he takes good care of his child whenever he's posting pics on his Facebook. At the end of the day, it's his own selfish way of controlling the *"narrative"* his delusional life to the outside world. He wants to give outsiders who are looking into his life, a false perception of his lack of fairy tale, wonderful father world. Behind closed doors, he could care less about his own child.

The narcissist if given the opportunity, will groom his child to have narcissistic tendencies as well. This means that your child will be put in abusive situations to cause division and chaos in other people's life. If the narcissist is in a new relationship, he will constantly use his child to make his new lover jealous. This is called *"**Triangulation**."*

The more resistance you give the narcissist, the more he/she will take it out on the child. For instance, if you deny the narcissist sex, you may not receive your regular child support payments. If you decide to start dating again, the narcissist will use the child to pry information about your whereabouts and if the child does not cooperate, the narcissist will discard the child. Again, it's all about control with the narcissist, but this time around, he's controlling you through the child. When your boundaries can't be violated, then the narcissist has no use for you, and if he cannot use the child to keep tabs, the child is useless as well. Know the game.

So no matter how wonderful the narcissist makes himself out to be as the "world's greatest parent" in front of his friends and family, he does NOT love his child. The child is only an extension of the narcissist and an innocent, naive pawn in the narcissist's sick chess game. The visitation must be supervised in order to protect the child from these types of divisive scenarios.

Don't try to force a relationship between your child and the narcissist down the line. You will regret it. The sooner you are able to get far away and protect the wellbeing of your child, the better off you will be. You will definitely struggle financially, but you will also have a sense of peace. You will be able to raise your child in a stable environment without the added drama from your ex. None of it is love. Just control and manipulation. Narcissists do not know how to love, nor will bringing a child into this world, change them into learning how. Let it go and move on. You can successfully raise your child on your own. If you are hell-bent on having another parental figure around, then seek out a mentor or pediatric therapist for your child in place of the narcissist's toxic parenting in your child's life.

CHAPTER 6

THE FAMILY COURT SYSTEM IS TOXIC AS HELL

One the most frustrating things about co-parenting with a narcissist is the exhausting process of filing for certain rights through family court. Nine times out of ten, as much as you try to avoid going to family court, the narcissist will deliberately derail your plans. Dysfunction is the only route that works for the narcissist and if you are not going to play by his rules, then he will drag his feet to make the entire situation that much more difficult for you.

Based on what city and state that you live in, when you are going through a divorce, you will have to more than likely ask your lawyer to put in writing, your requests for custody, visitation and child support. You can expect the narcissist to counter your claims just to drag the proceedings out longer. This is done out of spite to exert power and control over you. This is called "Litigation Abuse." Even though the narcissist is running a nasty smear campaign against you and telling everyone he can't wait to finalize the divorce, he's actually terrified of losing *permanent* control over you. So he will adjourn the court dates or delay signing off for as long as he can.

Family court on the other hand, will allow each parent to file for separate rights. The DNA testing must first be established to determine who the child belongs to. Once that is solidified, proceedings usually take place for custody, visitation and child support. Things can turn really volatile and nasty in family court because the narcissist despises you for establishing boundaries. You leave him no choice but to use the child to wage war against you.

When it comes to **custody**, the judge will likely favor the parent that takes care of the child 99% of the time (*usually the mother*). Because the father also has legal rights, he can request for joint custody (50/50). If things are really ugly, the narcissist will fight for sole custody and even bring false witnesses with him, like his mother or new lover, to testify against you to try to take your child away from you. The narcissist knows that the child is better off with you because he is a lousy parent, however, he knows if he can get at least joint custody, he can keep his foot in the doorway of your personal life. In a lot of cases, the narcissist will manage to convince the judge that the other parent is unfit. The judge will reverse the decision and grant sole custody to the narcissist which would allow him to further sue the other parent (you) for child support. This is why you must be vigilant in family court at all times when it comes to protecting your child.

Visitation can also be used as a bargaining chip if the narcissist wants to keep tabs on your life. Many of my clients told me that the narcissist would attempt to work out a schedule only to go against it to maintain the upper hand and have the custodial parent (you) running behind the narcissist to work things out on behalf of the child. Let me tell why you must go through family court to establish visitation, it's because the narcissist does not want to visit his child. Rather, he wants to use the child to visit **YOU**. That's right. When he's coming to visit and/or pick up his child, he's actually checking in to see what you've got going on in your life. He will also continue to triangulate you with his new lover, gaslight you and play mind games every chance he gets to have some sort of interaction with you. The only difference is, he will hide behind the mask of co-parenting. Visitation is a very risky ordeal because whether you realize it or not, the child is being emotionally abused every single time the narcissist picks him/her up for visitation. This is why I strongly encourage custodial parents to fight for "Supervised Visitation" to shut the narcissist down.

Supervised visitation is a mandated schedule put into action by the judge where the narcissistic parent must be monitored by a third party appointed by the judge at a set location when he comes to visit your child. The narcissist will despise you for doing this, but I can assure you, it's the only way to stop the narcissist from emotionally abusing your child and/or exposing your child to other abusers like his new lover, his family and toxic inner circle of friends. Trust me, when your back is turned, everyone except the narcissist, will be babysitting your child when the visitation isn't supervised. The narcissist doesn't want to care for his own child. If you want peace of mind, please request supervised visits and if the judge denies, you can appeal. Keep fighting and continue to document any inconsistencies of missed visits. It will seem unfair at times, but you must keep a constant paper trail of evidence. Eventually, the narcissist's lies will catch up to him.

If your child has any type of special needs such as Autism, ADHD and/or any other form of disability, don't expect the narcissist to be hands on with helping you. The narcissist wants the child to be disabled because as the child grows older, he/she will be easier to control and manipulate because of the disability. Sad but true. It is very critical that you find out firsthand who is around your child when you're not around. If you do not have supervised visitation and you allow your child to go alone with his/her narcissistic parent, then your child will definitely be triangulated with the new lover. What can possibly go wrong in this type of situation? Well if your ex is a narcissist and has already committed to toxic co-parenting, it will be even worse if his new lover is a narcissist as well because she will emotionally abuse your child as well during visitation.

Child Support, in my opinion, is a waste of time. If you are able to get any money out of the narcissist without a struggle, then go for it. If not, then don't even waste your time fighting for money in court. The narcissist is financially controlling and abusive. The ideal of him having to cough up money over to you, really pisses him off. He is fully aware that you have living expenses, food, utility and other bills that require help. He doesn't care about any of that. Every time he has to give you money, it means you're taking from something he deems important in his life. Whether it be a drug or alcohol addiction, gambling addiction or money for a romantic date with his new lover, he doesn't want you asking him for any financial help when it comes to the child. If the court is forced to garnish the narcissist's wages, he will hate you for it. Some have even quit their jobs to avoid paying child support and/or work "under the table" to wiggle their way out of monetary responsibilities.

Lastly, you're going to learn that your child's parent may not be the only one with Narcissistic Personality Disorder, there is a strong possibility that the judge may be one too. If your attorney is a court-appointed public defender, then he could be one as well. A lot of judge's favor the bad parent even if you present substantial evidence to show probable cause of toxic co-parenting. This is because the judge and attorneys are cut from the same cloth as your child's narcissistic parent is. All narcissists side with each other, even in the court of law. It's a very dangerous place for a child. There are lot cases where judges will award joint custody to the narcissistic parent and the child ends up molested or dead as a result of that judge's poor decision.

CHAPTER 7

YOU NARCISSISTIC IN-LAWS ARE TRASH

So you already know by now that your in-laws are fucking toxic as hell. You learned that before you became pregnant. Narcissists run in packs, so where there is one, there is usually a whole group of them right around the corner. When you were in a relationship with your ex, you saw different things that went on within his family. The in-laws are very messy, gossipy and two-faced. If your ex cheated on you, then you can rest assure that his shitty family already knew about it before you found out. In a lot of cases, the in-laws are already cool with the side chick. They will assist your ex with abusing you and then covering it up. They're all covert snakes.

Let me revert back to the last chapter where I discuss supervised visitation. The reason it is so critical to have supervised visits, is because your in-laws are also narcissistic and they will groom your child to also become narcissistic or either the scapegoat child of the family. All of your parenting will go out the window should your ex allow your child to be close knit to his family. They will work together to program your child to disrespect you. They will also gossip negatively about you in your child's presence, entertain the narcissist's side chicks in front of your child and exploit your child every chance they can get. Supervised visitation is mandatory. You're fighting up against an organized, dysfunctional family, and it is all set up to destroy you by using your child to control your life. Why do you think your ex turned out to be a piece of shit? Who do you think raised him? Where did he learn his toxic behaviors? That's right. He learned it from his narcissistic family. Please do not allow your child to visit their in-laws. Your in-laws will reinforce the emotional abuse and use your child to control you and work against you.

If the toxic in-laws insist that they want to see the child, it is best that you have them meet you on neutral grounds. Preferably a place like Chucky Cheese's or a family-oriented restaurant. Do not invite them into your home. You don't need that negative energy infesting your living space. These people are very demonic and they don't like you (*even if they pretend like they do*). Please remember that no matter how wrong your ex may be in this toxic situation, your in-laws will always side with him.

In this day and age, I always encourage my clients to gain as much knowledge about a potential partner's childhood upbringing as possible before engaging in sexual intercourse. The answers to who the narcissist is will reflect on the morals, standards and principles of his family. We have to be more selective with whom we marry and choose to have kids with. It's unfair to the child to have a toxic, demonic parent who lacks love and empathy. When you figure out that you're dealing with a narcissist, please do not rush to get married or have kids. You should be plotting your next escape. Trust me, you don't want to be locked down with an evil master manipulator for the next eighteen years. If you do happen to have children with a narcissist, please protect your children from his family. They are all abusive and will covertly groom your child to be another narcissist to add to their little organized army of dysfunction.

You have to remember that the overall goal of your narcissistic in-laws will be to constantly groom, recruit and control their children and grandchildren to keep the abuse contained within the family. They train their offspring to pass the dysfunction down from one generation to the next. Your children will be included if you are too laid back about their whereabouts when you allow the narcissist to take them for visitation. Please realize that the narcissist rarely watches his own children during his turn for visitation and he will likely dump your kids off on your in-laws or his side chicks; then the toxic brainwashing will begin. If you don't, you will run the risk of raising your children up to be narcissistic due to the constant exposure of being around your toxic in-laws. If your children become narcissists as they grow older, they will turn on you.

Take control of the entire situation and don't let your in-laws overstep your personal boundaries. They already know that the narcissist is a serial liar, cheater and abuser. They will still condone his behavior and turn the other cheek. Your in-laws are all very toxic and your children should not be exposed to their dysfunctional environment. The in-laws should only be allowed to see your children in an neutral public space where there are video cameras and witnesses. Do not leave your children alone with them.

CHAPTER 8

CHILD MOLESTATION & INCEST

I don't want to scare you, however, Narcissistic Personality Disorder must be explained in its entirety no matter how uncomfortable it may make you feel. In the first chapter, I explained what a narcissist is and why they target empathetic people. It's because they [narcissists] are on the constant prowl to seek narcissistic supply and they will take it from any source, including their own children.

Children are very innocent and the narcissist chooses to abuse them because they are easy targets. So please understand that the narcissist has the potential to molest your child and/or treat your child like a sexual object. The narcissist will also use your child to triangulate his other lovers when you're not around. This is very dangerous. (*Another reason why I feel that supervised visitation should be mandated*). The narcissist is fully capable of molesting your child or exposing your child to other narcissists who are also pedophiles.

Narcissists crave **"narcissistic supply"** like oxygen. It's a matter of life or death to them, so they don't care where they get it from. This is why you'll learn about your ex possibly being on the down low because in the heat of the moment, he will succumb to his sexual cravings. He is an addict and he doesn't care whether the supply comes from a male or female, just as long as he is getting his fix. The supply is like a drug to the narcissist and he will go crazy if he can't get his daily fix.

Please protect your children. If the narcissist does not molest your child, he will talk about very sexual inappropriate things in front of your child when you're not around, perform sexual acts in front of your child, drink/smoke drugs in front of your child and even watch porn in front of your child. When you think your ex is being a concerned and attentive parent, he is actually covertly abusing your child when you're not around. The narcissist will also coerce and intimidate your child into not telling you about what's going on to prevent you from taking action.

One other thing, if your ex is in a relationship with another narcissist, this is very dangerous for your child as well. The chances of your child being molested by the new lover, are very high. When two narcissists are in a relationship, it can be very dysfunctional and violent in front of the child. They do not care if they are exposing your child to toxicity because it was never about the child to begin with. Please monitor the visitation the best way possible and fight the court system until you get your way.

I am a victim of child molestation. My mother's second husband fondled me on multiple occasions when I was only fourteen years old. My mother went away to prison for four months and he took every opportunity to molest me while she was gone. When I had gathered up enough courage to tell her, she refused to believe me. I also told my father and he didn't do anything about it either. It was at that moment that I realized that both of my parents are narcissists because narcissists will side with other abusers. It is disgusting to know that I was living amongst a bunch of predators who took pleasure in covering up child molestation within the family. So I beg you to please monitor your child because narcissists can and will molest their own children. They will cover up their dirt because they have a circle of enablers willing to help them to sweep everything under the rug and paint you out to be the "crazy one" in the family. Please protect your babies from these predators! I beg you!

CHAPTER 9
CHILD ABUSE

As a victim of sexual molestation and child abuse, this is a very touchy subject for me. I remember growing up with a narcissistic mother and she allowing her second husband to get away with molesting me when I was a teenager. It took me several years to finally get up the courage to tell her about it, and when I did, she chose to believe his story over mine. I even confronted him to his face and called him a liar. The day that he fondled me, he came into my bedroom and thought I was sleep. I felt his dirty hands touch my ass and I had to pretend like I was waking up out of my sleep in order to scare him off. He did this repeatedly and he totally lied about it when he was called out.

He and my mother have been married for over 30 years now and I now see in hind sight that they are both narcissists. Two predators that feed off of each other's dysfunction and lies. They are both guilty for abusing me in my adolescent years.

In addition to the sexual abuse, I was also beaten badly by my mother. She would tie my hands and feet together with a scarf and strip my clothes and beat me with an extension cord. I have too many recollections of physical and verbal abuse involving my mother, that I have lost count. She was a demon in a dress. Her obsession with competing with me, destroying me and belittling me was a constant everyday thing in our household. I knew something was wrong with her, but I didn't know there was a name for this type of abuse. I didn't know anything about Narcissistic Personality Disorder.

I can remember a time that I was in high school; actually my senior year when she put a scar on my face. She got angry and hit me in the face with a curling iron near my eye. I went to school and walked around with my classmates asking me what happened. I had to lie to my classmates about the bruises to take the attention off of my face… until I ran into my guidance counselor in the hallway. She stopped me and asked me to step into her office where she interrogated me about the scar on my face. At first I was too scared to say anything, but I could tell she already knew. I guess being an educator, she was trained to spot child abuse in her students. I finally confessed and told her that my mother had hit me in the face and my guidance counselor proceeded to contact the Child Protective Services, while I sat in her office. My mother was investigated for child abuse and she was very nasty towards the social worker when they confronted her about it. This is one of many abuse stories at the hands of my narcissistic mother.

Another time where my mother abused me, I was around ten years old; she had beaten me so badly with a belt, I had welts all over my body. She sent me off to summer camp. I had a tank top on and all of the kids kept asking me why I had so many markings on my skin. It was so humiliating. She enjoyed embarrassing me and making me look ugly.

I have coached so many female victims who were molested by their stepfathers only to have their narcissistic mothers dismiss their accusations of sexual abuse. My female clients would tell me that their narcissistic mothers continued to stand by the side of the pedophile. It's a painful story that I have heard over and over again. Nothing hurts more than to know that your own mother and father refuse to protect you from other predators. Your narcissistic parents will sweep the family dirt underneath the rug and isolate you by calling you crazy and a liar.

Hear me when I tell you, if you allow your child to have visitation rights with the narcissist, you can rest assure that your child will be abused. How will your child be abused is the question. There are many forms of abuse and it also depends on the child's position in the narcissist's eyes. If the child is the scapegoat child, then the narcissist will punish the child much harder than the golden child of the family. The scapegoat child receives the brutal parts of abuse. Sexual, physical and financial abuse most of the time. The scapegoat child is also groomed to be the surrogate parent, caretaker, people-pleaser and doormat of the family. Now on the other hand, the golden child is the child who the narcissist deems innocent. The narcissist will usually spoil the golden child; compare and brag about this child to belittle the scapegoat child (triangulation). The narcissist will also coddle the golden child overlooking the child's bad behavior, rewarding the golden child with gifts and positive attention instead. The narcissist is basically grooming the golden child to become a *"narcissist-in-the-making"* as well. Whether it's the scapegoat child or either the golden child, both children are being abused by the narcissist.

Please realize that every time you allow your child to leave with the narcissist for visitation, your child will be subjected to different types of abuse in the presence of the narcissist, his family and also his new lover (*who more than likely is narcissistic as well*). This is why I stress that you fight for supervised visitation because you have no idea what your child is being exposed to when your child leaves for his weekend visits with the narcissist.

I beg you to please take a vigilant stance on protecting your child from being alone with the narcissist. In many cases, children have **DIED** at the hands of their narcissistic parent during a regular weekend visit, to spite the other parent. We must take child abuse serious and take preventive measures to make sure our children are safeguarded from potential harm.

CHAPTER 10
CO-PARENTING APPS

With today's inventions in technology, we are seeing a surge in new applications everywhere. A new wave of apps were created to maintain the peace between two people who share custody of a child, are now being used in the family court system as evidence. Both parents have to download the app onto their phone and communicate with each other in regards to visitation, financial needs and the overall well-being of the child. It also serves to document the consistent behavior of the non-custodial parent in addition to tracking both parents' responsibilities pertaining to the child. Unfortunately, this is very detrimental to the narcissist. I will tell you why.

Before the co-parent app was introduced, we had to rely on phone calls, text messages and email to communicate with the very difficult narcissist. When dealing with a narcissist, you already know that communication is very sporadic, inconsistent and full of gas-lighting when trying to discuss matters of co-parenting. The narcissist makes it extremely difficult when discussing his role in co-parenting. He doesn't want to come to an agreement that serves the benefit of the child because he is well aware that he is not in it for the child to begin with.

He basically enjoys using the child as an excuse to contact and/or communicate with you. Once he connects with you, the subject will switch from the child's needs, to your personal life. The narcissist will keep tabs on your life every time he interacts with you, using the child as a pawn to connect. He will even go as far as Face Time you while his new lover is sitting right next to him in order to triangulate you both and punish you. This form of communication is proven to be abusive so the co-parenting app shuts all of that bullshit down.

The narcissist will hate using the co-parenting app, but you still need to demand that the family courts enforce it in your custody/visitation petition. The judge can monitor and track all of the correspondence and the narcissist can't wiggle his way out of his responsibilities. Outside of hiring a private investigator, this is the only way you can catch the narcissist red-handed, by maintaining a constant paper trail of documented evidence. If all communication regarding the child is documented through the app, it allows the narcissist little room to be inconsistent or irresponsible unless he chooses to discard the child altogether.

Please demand that the family court system enforces the app. Change your phone number so the narcissist cannot Face Time you, video chat, text or call you from fake burner numbers. Reinforce your boundaries and make him respect your personal space. He won't like the app one bit, but that's not your problem. Put the focus back on co-parenting and take your power back from the narcissist. He has no business asking you about your personal life. He will continue to overstep his boundaries if you allow it.

Again, as I stated earlier, the only reason the narcissist has children, is to solely trap you into submission and control. The child serves as a pawn piece that will forever connect you and bind you to the narcissist. The child becomes the secondary victim in the picture. Because of the stipulations and legalities of the family court system, you have to cope with more emotional abuse because you can't escape the narcissist due to his parental rights. The narcissist will use his child to confront you knowing that you can't deny him access by law. This is why the family court system is so flawed because it enables abusers to constantly interact with victims and children. The family court system doesn't do enough to protect children from harmful narcissistic abuse.

CHAPTER 11

DOMESTIC VIOLENCE (ESCAPING YOUR ABUSER)

What's so heartbreaking is the fact that most narcissists are walking around undiagnosed with ASPD (Anti-Social Personality Disorder). A Narcopath (*a narcissist who is also a sociopath/ psychopath*) is fully capable of committing violence in his own home and he will attack everyone, including his children. He has a violent temper and an "*above the law*" attitude that overtly defies law enforcement. As long as nobody is looking, he feels that he can get away with assaulting, strangling, cursing, belittling, torturing and even murdering his spouse and kids.

One of the hardest things to do is leave an abusive man for good. When you have children involved and you're trying to escape, you are bombarded with obstacles that hinder you from leaving. Narcissists are financially controlling so you may not have enough money saved up to make sure your kids are fed should you decide to leave. You don't have a place to stay and the women's shelters are full. You can't call on your family members because you don't want them gossiping about your hardships and/or alerting your abuser of your exit plans. You're isolated from the world and you don't know what to do.

Let me just speak from my own experience. I've been there and done that. I couldn't call on my family or friends. I didn't have anywhere to run. My abuser had me isolated and too afraid to tell anyone. He was very controlling and kept a large knife with him to intimidate me. I prayed for a way out because my finances were low and I didn't have a car at the time.

It wasn't until I was forced into a corner which left me no choice but to leave or else I would end up dead. It was a cold night in the Bronx during the winter. Me and my daughter were asleep in the bed and my ex-husband was in the living room getting high with his friend. I had to go to work in the morning, so I was already asleep when he and his friend started up their partying. I had locked the bedroom door and dozed off. In the middle of the night, he tried to come in and I told him to go sleep on the couch (*he's violent when he gets high*).

He begged me to open the door and he promised me that he would lie down and go to sleep. I opened the door and he began attacking me. He then proceeded to drag me into the other room where he continued punching me in the head. My daughter woke up and was frightened. It was at that moment that he punched me directly in my eye. I could feel the swelling and my eye completely closed up. I screamed in pain. He then ran into the kitchen and began searching for a knife. At that moment I knew if I didn't run and get help, he was going to kill me. So I ran out the front door with only a tank top and panties on. The wind chill was below 15 degrees and I couldn't feel it because my adrenaline was running high. I screamed for help until a group of young men saw me and ran into the house. They began beating up my ex and they pinned him down until the police arrived. He was arrested and charged with battery and child endangerment. I was taken to the hospital and treated for a broken eye socket.

Me and my daughter ended up in a domestic violence shelter and I continued to go to work. It was hard. There were days I would have to take my daughter to work with me, but we got through it. What made things difficult was the constant stalking. My ex continued to follow me at my job. He broke the restraining order four different times. He was in a new relationship and still continued to stalk. I had him thrown in jail and it had to take the judge threatening him with five years of prison in Rikers Island, to get him to leave me alone.

I say all of this to say, if you're in a situation where you and your children are in a violent environment, please take the clothes on your back and leave. Don't wait to save up money. Don't save your clothes. Plan an exit strategy. Gather your children's school records, birth certificates, driver's license, life insurance, etc., and get the fuck out of there. Catch a Greyhound bus and go to another city. If you fear that your ex is going to press charges for parental kidnapping, do not leave the state, but do travel to another county within the state. Call various homeless shelters until one finds a bed for you and your kids. Nobody said it would be easy, but struggling is better than the police scraping your dead body off of the ground. Your children have been exposed to enough abuse. It's time to do something about it. Stop procrastinating and put together an exit strategy. The resources are out there, are you vigilant enough to fight for it? Your partner can't be in the house 24/7. He has to go to work, so you need to escape while he's gone. God bless you. ☺

DIRECTORY OF RESOURCES
A-Z

DIRECTORY OF RESOURCES

National Domestic Violence Hotline
thehotline.org
800-199-7233

The Legal Aid Society
legalaidnyc.org
212-577-3300

National Resource Center on Domestic Violence
nrcdv.org
800-537-2238

RAINN
rainn.org
800-656-4673

Love is Respect
866-331-9474

Alabama
Alabama Coalition Against Domestic Violence
www.acadv.org

King's Home
www.kingshome.com

YWCA Central Alabama
www.ywcabham.org/community-housing

United Way of Central Alabama
www.uwca.org/oasis-counseling-women-children

Alaska

Alaska Network on Domestic Violence & Sexual Assault
www.andvsa.org

Fairbanks Native Association
www.fairbanksnative.org/our-services

Alaska Family Services
www.akafs.org

Clare House
www.cssalaska.org/our-programs/clare-house

Arizona

Arizona Department of Economic Security
www.des.az.gov

Sojourner Center
www.sojournercenter.org

Hope Women's Center
www.hopewomenscenter.org

Arkansas

Women and Children First
www.wcfarkansas.org

Arkansas Baptist Children's Homes & Family Ministries
www.arkansasfamilies.org

Methodist Family Health
www.methodistfamily.org

Conway Women's Shelter
www.conwaywomensshelter.com

California

California Partnership to End Domestic Violence
www.cpedv.org/domestic-violence-organizations-california

Immigration Center for Women and Children
www.icwclaw.org

Aviva
www.aviva.org

Contra Costa Health Services
www.cchealth.org/fmch/ccs.php

Alta California Regional Center
www.altaregional.org

Family Voices of California
www.familyvoicesofca.org

Neighborhood Legal Services of Los Angeles County
www.nlsla.org/contact_domestic.php

Jewish Family Service LA
www.jfsla.org

Haven Hills
www.havenhills.org

Colorado
Colorado Department of Human Services
www.cdhs.colorado.gov/our-services/child-and-family-services

House of Hope
www.thefamilytree.org/house-hope

The Gathering Place
www.tgpdenver.org

The Women's Foundation of Colorado
www.wfco.org

Mary's Home
www.dreamcenters.com/marys-home

Safe House Denver
www.safehouse-denver.org

Colorado Crisis Services
www.coloradocrisisservices.org

Connecticut
Connecticut Coalition Against Domestic Violence
www.ctcadv.org

Women and Families Center
www.womenfamilies.org

The Connection
www.theconnectioninc.org/family-support-services

Women and Family Life Center
www.womenandfamilylife.org

Delaware
Delaware Coalition Against Domestic Violence
www.dcadv.org

Child Inc.
www.childinc.com

Help is Here
www.helpisherede.com

Florida
Florida Department of Children & Families
www.myflfamilies.com/service-programs/domestic-violence/map.shtml

Florida Department of Children & Families
www.myflfamilies.com/service-programs/access

Miami Rescue Mission
www.miamirescuemission.com/women.htm

One Heart for Women and Children
www.oneheartforwomenandchildren.org

Women in Distress
www.womenindistress.org

The Shelter for Abused Women & Children
www.naplesshelter.org

Broward Outreach Center
www.browardoutreachcenter.org

Georgia
Georgia Coalition Against Domestic Violence

www.gcadv.org

Division of Family & Children Services
www.dfcs.georgia.gov

Safe Haven Transitional
www.safehaventransitional.org

Atlanta Day Shelter for Women & Children
www.atlantamission.org/atlanta-day-shelter

Hospitality House for Women
www.hospitalityhouseforwomen.org

Atlanta Mission
www.atlantamission.org

Anna Crawford Children's Center
www.cherokeechildadvocates.org

Atlanta Children's Shelter
www.acsatl.org

Women to the World
www.womentotheworld.org

Hawaii
Parents & Children Together

www.pacthawaii.org/our-work/domestic-violence-prevention/ohia

Oahu Family Peace Center
www.pacthawaii.org

The Institute for Human Services
www.ihshawaii.org

Idaho
Idaho Council on Domestic Violence & Victim Assistance
www.icdv.idaho.gov

Women and Children's Alliance
www.wcaboise.org

Boise Rescue Mission Ministries
www.boiserm.org/services/women-children

Illinois
Illinois Coalition Against Domestic Violence
www.ilcadv.org

Primo Center
www.primocenter.org

Connections for Abused Women and Their Children

www.cawc.org

Family Rescue
www.familyrescueinc.org

Life Spring
www.waysidecross.org/lifespringwomenshelter

Deborah's Place
www.deborahsplace.org

Indiana
Indiana Coalition Against Domestic Violence
www.icadvinc.org

Wheeler Mission
www.wheelermission.org

Children's Bureau
www.childrensbureau.org

Coburn Place
www.coburnplace.org

Dayspring Center
www.dayspringindy.org

Iowa

Iowa Coalition Against Domestic Violence
www.icadv.org

Children and Families of Iowa
www.cfiowa.org

Waypoint Services
www.waypointservices.org

Hope Center for Women and Children
www.hopeiowa.org

Kansas
Kansas Coalition Against Sexual & Domestic Violence
www.kcsdv.org

City Union Mission
www.cityunionmission.org/women-and-family

Hope House
www.hopehouse.net

Kentucky
Kentucky Coalition Against Domestic Violence
www.kcadv.org

The Center for Women and Families
www.thecenteronline.org

Up for Women and Children
www.uplouisville.org

Louisiana
Louisiana Coalition Against Domestic Violence
www.lcadv.org

Iris Domestic Violence Center
www.stopdv.org

Women's Children's Center for Mental Wellness
www.wccmw.com

New Orleans Women and Children's Center
www.nowcs.org

Maine
The Maine Coalition to End Domestic Violence
www.mcedv.org

Crossroads
www.crossroadsme.org

Pines Health Center
www.pineshealth.org

Infinity House

www.wellspringmaine.com/programs/infinity-house-women-children-residential

Maryland
Maryland Network Against Domestic Violence
www.mnadv.org

Springboard Community Services
www.springboardmd.org

Catholic Charities
www.catholiccharities-md.org

House of Ruth Maryland
www.hruth.org

Baltimore Outreach Services
www.baltimoreoutreach.org

Massachusetts
Casa Myrna
www.casamyrna.org

St. Mary's Center for Women and Children
www.stmaryscenterma.org

Abby's House
www.abbyshouse.org

Rosie's Place
www.rosiesplace.org

Michigan
Michigan Coalition to End Domestic & Sexual Violence
www.mcedsv.org

Child and Family Charities
www.childandfamily.org

Eve's Place
www.eveinc.org

Minnesota
Violence Free Minnesota
www.vfmn.org

RS Eden
www.rseden.org

Wellcome Manor Family Services
www.wellcomemanor.org

Wayside Recovery Center
www.waysiderecovery.org

Mississippi
Mississippi Coalition Against Domestic Violence

www.mcadv.org

Gulf Coast Center for Nonviolence
www.gccfn.org/wordpress/programs

United Way of Southeast Mississippi
www.unitedwaysems.org/DAFS

Care Lodge
www.carelodge.com

Missouri
Missouri Coalition Against Domestic & Sexual Violence
www.mocadsv.org

ALIVE
www.alivestl.org

Montana
Montana Coalition Against Domestic & Sexual Violence
www.mcadsv.com

YWCA of Missoula
www.ywcaofmissoula.org/services/domestic-violence

Community Support Center
www.cscofswmt.org/montana-resources.html

Nebraska

Nebraska Coalition to End Sexual & Domestic Violence
www.nebraskacoalition.org

Women's Center for Advancement
www.wcaomaha.org

Heartland Family Service
www.heartlandfamilyservice.org

Nevada
Nevada Coalition to End Domestic & Sexual Violence
www.ncedsv.org

Domestic Violence Resource Center
www.domesticviolenceresourcecenter.org

Women and Children's Center of the Sierra
www.waccs.org

Safe Nest
www.safenest.org

New Hampshire
New Hampshire Coalition Against Domestic & Sexual
Violence
www.nhcadsv.org

New Beginnings Without Violence and Abuse

www.newbeginningsnh.org

Crisis Center of Central New Hampshire
www.cccnh.org

New Hampshire Charitable Foundation
www.nhcf.org

New Jersey
New Jersey Coalition to End Domestic Violence
www.njcedv.org

Center for Hope and Safety
www.hopeandsafetynj.org

YWCA Northern New Jersey
www.ywcannj.org/healingspace

Catholic Charities of Trenton
www.catholiccharitiestrenton.org/domestic-violence-services

Contact Organization
www.contactburlco.org

Jersey Battered Women's Services
www.jbws.org

180 Turning Lives Around

www.180nj.org

Jewish Family Services Women's Center
www.jfsmiddlesex.org/womens-center

Women Aware
www.womenaware.net

Passaic County Women's Center
www.passaiccountywomenscenter.org

Oasis
www.oasisnj.org

New Mexico
New Mexico Coalition Against Domestic Violence
www.nmcadv.org

New Mexico Children, Youth & Families Department
www.cyfd.org/domestic-violence

Albuquerque Family Advocacy Center
www.cabq.gov/albuquerque-family-advocacy-center

DVRC
WWW.dvrcnm.org

Women's Housing Coalition
www.womenshousingcoalition.com

New York
New York State Coalition Against Domestic Violence
www.nyscadv.org

Survive To Thrive Global
www.survivetothriveglobal.org

Safe Horizon
www.safehorizon.org

NYC Center Against Domestic Violence
www.nycservice.org/organizations/1812

WNY Women's Foundation
www.wnywomensfoundation.org

Urban Resource Institute
www.urinyc.org

Center for the Women of New York
www.cwny.org

New York Center for Children
www.newyorkcenterforchildren.org

North Carolina

North Carolina Coalition Against Domestic Violence
www.nccadv.org

Safe Alliance
www.safealliance.org

Coastal Women's Shelter
www.coastalwomensshelter.org

Jamie Kimble Foundation for Courage
www.jkffc.org/resources/hotlines-shelters

North Dakota
Domestic Violence Crisis Center
www.courage4change.org

CAWS North Dakota
www.cawsnorthdakota.org

Family Crisis Shelter
www.familycrisisshelter.com

Ohio
Action Ohio Coalition for Battered Women
www.actionohio.org

Ohio Domestic Violence Network
www.odvn.org

Oklahoma
Oklahoma Coalition Against Domestic Violence and Sexual
Assault
www.ocadvsa.org

YWCA Oklahoma
www.ywcaokc.org/domestic-violence

The Chicksaw Nation
www.chickasaw.net/Services/Domestic-Violence-Services

Oregon
Oregon Coalition Against Domestic and Sexual Violence
www.ocadsv.com

Clackamas Women's Services
www.cwsor.org

Pennsylvania
Pennsylvania Coalition Against Domestic Violence
www.pcadv.org

Women Against Abuse
www.womenagainstabuse.org

YWCA Harrisburg

www.ywcahbg.org

The Women's Center
www.thewomenscenterinc.org

Safe Berks
www.safeberks.org

Third Street Alliance
www.thirdstreetalliance.org

Women In Transition
www.helpwomen.org

Puerto Rico
The Office of Women Advocates
Box 11382
Fernandez Juancus Station
Santurce, PR 00910
(787) 721-7676 Fax: (787) 725-9248

Rhode Island
Rhode Island Coalition Against Domestic Violence
www.ricadv.org

Help Line Rhode Island
www.helplineri.com/domestic-violence

Women's Center of Rhode Island

www.womenscenterri.org

Cross Roads Rhode Island
www.crossroadsri.org

South Carolina
South Carolina Coalition Against Domestic Violence and
Sexual Assault
www.sccadvasa.org

Sister Care
www.sistercare.org

Safe Passage
www.safepassagesc.org

Safe Harbor
www.safeharborsc.org

South Dakota
South Dakota Coalition Against Domestic Violence & Sexual
Assault
www.sdcedsv.org

Children's Inn
www.chssd.org/childrensinn

Safe Harbor
www.safeharborsd.org

Tennessee
Tennessee Coalition Against Domestic & Sexual Violence
www.tncoalition.org

Domestic Violence Sexual Assault Center
www.dvsacenter.org

Women Are Safe
www.womenaresafe.org

Safe Space
www.safespacetn.org

Texas
Texas Council On Family Violence
www.tcfv.org

Family Services of Southern Texas
www.westrengthenfamilies.org

Hays-Caldwell Women's Center
www.hcwc.org

Families to Freedom
www.familiestofreedom.org

Genesis Women's Shelter
www.genesisshelter.org

Family Violence Prevention Services
www.fvps.org

Utah
Utah Domestic Violence Coalition
www.udvc.org

YWCA Utah
www.ywcautah.org/what-we-do/safety

Safe Harbor
www.safeharborhope.org

Volunteers of America
www.voaut.org/cwc

Virgin Islands
Virgin Islands Domestic Violence and Sexual Assault Council
4100 Sion Farm Shopping Center
St. Croix, VI 00822
(340) 719-0144 Fax: (340) 719-5521
www.vidvsac.org

Vermont
Vermont Network Against Domestic Violence and Sexual
Assault
www.vtnetwork.org

Steps to End Domestic Violence
www.stepsvt.org

Commission on Women
www.women.vermont.gov/Violence

Circle VT
www.circlevt.org

Virginia
Virginia Sexual & Domestic Violence Action Alliance
www.vsdvalliance.org

Avalon Center
www.avaloncenter.org

Doorways VA
www.doorwaysva.org/get-help/domestic-violence-resources

YWCA Central Virginia
www.ywcacva.org

Bethany House of Northern Virginia
www.bhnv.org

Washington
Washington State Coalition Against Domestic Violence
www.wscadv.org

Washington State Native American Coalition Against
Domestic and Sexual Assault
www.womenspirit.net

West Virginia
West Virginia Coalition Against Domestic Violence
www.wvcadv.org

Eastern Panhandle Empowerment Center
www.epecwv.org

Wisconsin
End Domestic Abuse Wisconsin: The Wisconsin Coalition
Against Domestic Violence
www.endabusewi.org

End Domestic Abuse
www.endabusewi.org

Women and Children's Horizons
www.wchkenosha.org

Wyoming
Wyoming Coalition Against Domestic Violence and Sexual
Assault
www.wyomingdvsa.org

Crisis Intervention Services
www.cis-park.org

Protecting the Pawn: Co-Parenting with a Narcissist